Original title:
A House Full of Green

Copyright © 2025 Creative Arts Management OÜ
All rights reserved.

Author: Tobias Sterling
ISBN HARDBACK: 978-1-80581-935-6
ISBN PAPERBACK: 978-1-80581-462-7
ISBN EBOOK: 978-1-80581-935-6

Serene Sanctum of Nature

In corners where plants seem to plot,
They dance when the sunlight hits the spot.
A cactus giving side-eye to a fern,
Sassy leaves with secrets they discern.

The ferns are gossiping with the trees,
Joking about how to catch the breeze.
A squirrel trips on a vine with flair,
Nature's laugh is rich, beyond compare.

The Leafy Refuge

A parrot thinks it owns the whole place,
While a spider spins webs with a grin on its face.
Lizards having tea on the window sill,
Chirping their secrets, what a thrill!

The ivy creeps up, a sneaky prank,
Deciding to hide the poor gardener's tank.
With every leaf, a new story unfolds,
As laughter in nature is bold and gold.

Whispers of Verdant Walls

The wallflowers giggle at blooming pride,
As the daisies argue who will be the guide.
In this green kingdom, friendships twist and twine,
With flower power brewing like a fine wine.

Every petal has a tale to tell,
In a plot full of puns, all is well.
A rogue little weed throws a party tonight,
Under the moon, it dances with delight.

The Lush Embrace

In this jungle of joy, I take my seat,
Where worms recount stories, so bittersweet.
The daisies tease the roses in a jest,
While mushrooms play charades, passing the test.

The bamboo sways as it loses its cool,
And the slugs make a splash in the garden pool.
With laughs echoing under leafy awnings,
Nature's charm is like early dawnings.

In the Shade of Memories

In corners where the laughter grew,
The cat wore leaves like a hat, it's true.
We danced around the blooming thyme,
While ants joined in, keeping time.

The vines laughed as we tripped on roots,
Wearing garden gloves like silly boots.
We tossed the weeds, they tossed us back,
And squirrels plotted their own attack.

Green Hues of Comfort

In every pot, a tale's untold,
Plants whisper secrets, brave and bold.
The basil's busy making plans,
While mint thinks it can outsmart the cans.

The daisies giggle, petals wide,
While gnomes waltz with so much pride.
We sip our drinks, smiles on our face,
As ladybugs win the race for space.

Breezes through Garden Corners

The wind plays tricks, it steals my hat,
As butterflies flit where the lilies sat.
I chase after, with joy and glee,
While bees engage in a raucous spree.

The fence creaks like it knows a joke,
As I tussle with a stubborn oak.
In every breeze's playful cheer,
I swear the garden grins ear to ear.

Sunlight Filtering Through Canopies

The sunbeams dance on leaves above,
As shadows play in the game of 'love.'
My hat's a shelter, a leafy dome,
As squirrels march like they own the home.

Giggling flowers gossip sweet,
The tomatoes flash their juicy meat.
We dine on salad, fresh and bright,
With dressing made from dreams of light.

Botanical Sleep

Plants snore softly, I must confess,
With leaves that rustle in leafy dress.
Laughter bubbles from a pot so bright,
As cacti giggle in the pale moonlight.

The spider plant spins tales of the day,
While ferns shake their heads, 'Oh, what a way!'
Dormant dreams where vines waltz with ease,
In a garden slumber, a leafy tease.

Sun-Dappled Retreats

Sunbeams bounce on the potted crowd,
While leaves play peekaboo, soft and loud.
A rubber plant claims its regal chair,
Declaring, 'You can't sit here, beware!'

The orchids chuckle at the tangled rose,
With petals whispering secrets no one knows.
Fern fronds dance, flaunting their sway,
In this crazy jungle, come out and play!

The Foliage's Gentle Mirth

Jade laughs boldly, a treasure untold,
As thyme keeps secrets of dreams bold and old.
Succulents wink, with a mischievous grin,
Sipping on sunshine, where antics begin.

Pothos sprawls with dramatic flair,
While basil plots with a scent to share.
In each little corner, a joke lands hard,
Garden gales echo, fun on guard.

Nature's Requiem in Rooms

In the stillness, there's chatter to hear,
From daisies gossiping, spreading good cheer.
A fern plays the violin, nature's sweet sound,
Creating a symphony where giggles abound.

The geraniums giggle, a riotous scene,
While a wandering vine drapes in between.
They sing lullabies to the pets on the floor,
In this leafy haven, who could ask for more?

Roots that Bind Us Together

In the yard, the weeds have grown,
Each one a plant, like a dog with a bone.
They argue and fight for sunlit space,
A tussle that's quite an amusing race.

When one gets tall, the others frown,
It's a leafy scrimmage all over town.
The squirrels join in, they cheer and jeer,
Who knew plants had feelings, my dear!

The Tapestry of Green Life

The ivy climbed higher, what a sight,
It thinks it's a bird, taking flight.
The ferns make faces, swaying with glee,
Telling tales of the breeze, oh so free.

A cactus cracks jokes, it's sharp but it's funny,
While the daisies giggle, looking sunny.
In this great green show, all are a part,
Who knew plant life could be so smart?

Blessings from the Herb Garden

Thyme sings to basil, oh what a tune,
While mint rolls its eyes, like a cranky balloon.
They spice up the air with stories old,
Of cooking escapades, brave and bold.

The rosemary jests, 'I'm the queen of the pot!'
While sage, not to budge, says, 'No, I am hot!'
A blend of laughter, they stir and they sway,
In this fragrant fest, they dance all day!

Enchanted by Foliage

The leaves play chess with the playful breeze,
Trading places with grand ease.
The sun peeks in, with a wink and a grin,
As the grass does a jig, let the fun begin!

The clover's a jester, with tricks up its sleeve,
Making the daisies gasp and believe.
In this green wonderland, laughter doth ring,
Who knew that plants could love to sing?

Dreaming Amidst Leaves

In rooms where vines like snakes do creep,
I swear the ferns talk in their sleep.
The potted plants throw lively shade,
I caught a cactus in a charade.

The orchid spritzed me, oh so spry,
While gaggles of daisies winked, oh my!
I tripped on ivy, did a dance,
That green stuff really knows how to prance.

A vine swings low, then leaps with style,
While leafy friends share a cheeky smile.
In this fun jungle, every turn,
I find new quirks and lessons to learn.

The Whispering Woods

In corners where the moss now plays,
I heard the whispers of tiny days.
The curtains swayed with a giggling breeze,
And knocked over plants like a fit of tease.

A sunflower blinks, then hits the floor,
Its secret? It wants to join the floor's tour!
With tales of roots that dig and delve,
They formed a club, forgot about themselves.

So when you hear the rustle and cheer,
Just know those greens are plotting here.
A forest in your living space,
You can't escape this leafy embrace.

Petals in the Hallway

A rose in the hallway wore a bow,
It's throwing a party, don't you know?
The violets wink, inviting all,
While tulips giggle with a floral ball.

Forget the guests; the petals insist,
That plants can groove; they can't be missed!
When lilies sway to their own sweet tune,
You'll see tulips cutting up the room.

The daisies dance in a joyful trance,
While potted succulents flex their stance.
In this quirky hall where laughter brews,
Nature's got moves; who needs a muse?

Nature's Breath in Every Room

In every nook, a fern has grown,
It's formed a band, and you're the loan.
The peace lily sings, quite off-key,
While cacti cheer with spiny glee.

The mint leaves gossip in the air,
While ivy sneaks a hidden dare.
"Who ordered a salad?" a rubber tree yells,
As the tomatoes chuckle, sharing their spells.

The basil spritzes, gives a pep talk,
While all the herbs form an outside block.
So join the shindig, oh don't be shy,
With laughter and greens, we'll surely fly.

Vibrance of the Natural Realm

In my garden, plants conspire,
To dress the place in leafy attire.
The cactus jokes, 'I'm the sharpest here,'
While daisies giggle, 'We bring the cheer!'

The ferns are throwing a dance in a pot,
They sway to the rhythm, like dancers hot.
The herbs chime in with a herbal refrain,
'We're cooking up fun, forget the mundane!'

The flowers gossip, wearing bright hues,
'Have you heard the news? The weeds wear shoes!'
But every petal plays a part in the show,
In this vibrant realm, each plant steals the glow.

With every dusk, the critters will glean,
In this riotous state, it's quite the scene!
Nature's folly reigns, full of delight,
In this verdant joke, we laugh through the night.

The Sanctuary of Leaf and Bloom

In a patch where laughter meets bright green leaves,
Lies a sanctuary of joy, where nature weaves.
The flowers wear hats made of sunbeam gold,
And the vines spin tales that never get old.

The daisies play cards, the violets bake pie,
'What's the secret?' the roses will slyly imply.
The sunflowers laugh, 'We're tall for a reason,
To spot all the fun in this grand garden season!'

The tomatoes roll dice, they're betting on rain,
While peas in their pods make a joke about grain.
Every leaf is a whisper, every sprout a song,
In this quirky realm, you just can't go wrong!

As night brings a chill, the crickets will croon,
While the fireflies shine like miniature moons.
In their sanctuary formed by nature's own hand,
The laughter of flora makes life so unplanned.

Essence of the Green Retreat

Welcome to the retreat of the chlorophyll crew,
Where the broccoli jokes and the lettuce sings too.
The spinach wears glasses, claiming it's wise,
While the radishes wait, with mischievous eyes.

The daisies debate who's the fairest of all,
While tulips declare they're having a ball.
Oh, how they giggle, these petal-clad fools,
Dancing in gardens, breaking all rules!

The thyme and the sage conspire in glee,
Plotting to overthrow the herb called parsley.
In this lively brawl of fun and good cheer,
Each plant has a story that we're glad to hear.

As dusk drapes a veil on the mischief and play,
The flora will whisper, 'Let's do this each day!'
With joy in their roots, and love in the air,
In this green retreat, life's jokes are laid bare.

The Garden's Chorus

In the garden, the veggies scheme,
Dancing carrots and a broccoli dream.
Tomato's red, but oh so shy,
Whispers to radishes passing by.

The sunflowers giggle at the bees,
While lettuce flirts with the gentle breeze.
Cabbages roll in a leafy race,
As herbs make a splash with their zesty grace.

Morning glories stretch and yawn,
While peas play tag on the grassy lawn.
Zucchini jokes in the summer's glow,
Who knew a vegetable could steal the show?

Each vine sings out a silly tune,
Under the watch of the charming moon.
So come and join this leafy spree,
In the garden's laughter, wild and free.

Verdant Corners of Solitude

In a bright corner where the ferns hide,
A timid snail took a bold ride.
With a shell that sparkles like a gem,
He dreams of joining the firefly den.

On a branch, a parrot tells a joke,
While nearby, a grumpy old oak.
"Why did the flower refuse to dance?"
"Because it found romance in a ladybug's pants!"

A curious frog leaps without a care,
While a shy tulip whispers, 'Oh, beware!'
Mice munch popcorn under moonlight's beam,
Plotting pranks like a delightful dream.

So sneak a peek in this funny nook,
Where every leaf has a giggling book.
Nature's corners are never mute,
They hum with laughter in a leafy suit.

A Treetop's Whisper

High in the treetops, squirrels convene,
Chattering loudly, as if they're a team.
With acorns tossed in a playful brawl,
They argue which nut is the best for the fall.

A crow caws loudly with a knowing grin,
"Let's hold a contest! Who'll win this spin?"
But the woodpecker drums a silly beat,
Declaring, "A dance-off would be quite neat!"

The branches sway with a giggling breeze,
As sparrows gossip with the greatest of ease.
Frolicking leaves join in the fun,
Chasing the shadows, avoiding the sun.

So if you look up at the tree so tall,
You might hear laughter amidst it all.
Nature's jests not hidden but bright,
In the treetops' whispers under the light.

Leaves that Tell Tales

In autumn's grip, the leaves start to chatter,
Telling stories of what made them scatter.
"Oh, the wind swept me up for a spin,
And there I danced with a cheeky tin!"

One leaf recalls a day so grand,
When a child caught it right in her hand.
"But it tickled and teased, so off I flew,
To play with the clouds and drop from the blue!"

Amongst the branches, a tale's at play,
Of crickets who sing and twirl all day.
"Join us!" they chirp, "It's all in good cheer,
Just watch for the cat, he's lurking near!"

So gather 'round for the leaf's escapade,
With chuckles that float in the afternoon glade.
Every rustle is laughter, every fall a delight,
In the leafy collections of joy, day and night.

Serene Sanctuary of Foliage

In corners where the vines like to creep,
A sleepy cat finds a leafy heap.
Wandering gnomes with their hats askew,
Throwing shade on the plants they brew.

Ferns dance wildly when wind comes to play,
Chasing dust bunnies that scurry away.
Potted pals whisper secrets at night,
As the moon gives the garden its light.

Lettuce leaves gossip, oh what a thrill,
While daisies argue over the best hill.
A squirrel in rubber boots and a grin,
Checks on the carrots to see if they win.

Every day's a party, just look around,
When the tulips wear crowns and spin round.
Nature's laughter fills the air with glee,
In this green circus, we're all so free!

Nature's Breath of Fresh Air

The basil's got flavor, but so does the thyme,
They argue about dinner, both think they're prime.
While onions peel back layers, shedding a tear,
Potatoes laugh loudly, 'We'll steal the show here!'

A cactus stands proud with its prickly attire,
Swaying with pride like a potted empire.
The herbs hold a meeting to plan for a feast,
While wise old oak chuckles, 'Let's bring the yeast!'

In sunlit spots, critters play catch and tease,
Rabbits wear sunglasses, lounging with ease.
The peppers are spicy, but still need a hand,
They need help with salsa, a dance so unplanned.

Birds chirp out scores to this quirky play,
While the clouds float by, bringing rain to obey.
A playful breeze tickles all that it can,
This garden's a fun zone, every beast and man!

The Lush Symphony

Among the leaves, a symphony plays,
Worms tap their toes, dancing in praise.
Living violins strum on the breeze,
While trumpets of tulips create melodies.

The daisies hold hands singing in tune,
While a porcupine strums a song to the moon.
A woodpecker's beat is both funny and bold,
As the sun hovers high, this spectacle unfolds.

Skunks join the chorus with scents so divine,
While squirrels juggle acorns, all in good time.
This vibrant ensemble of creatures and greens,
Makes every day feel like a big movie scene.

So if you should wander into this blend,
Expect the unexpected, round every bend.
The melody here is sweet but so strange,
In nature's own patch, there's always a change!

Rebirth Through Greenery

Beneath the soil, a party's begun,
Seeds tell tales of their winter run.
Each sprout flips and flops, eager to see,
The bright new world in which it will be.

Beetles wear hats made of dandelion,
While caterpillars sing, blissfully tryin'.
The sunflowers tower, thinking they know best,
While zucchini checks in on the whole garden fest.

The breeze carries giggles through gardens galore,
As daisies provide comfy seats for the floor.
Each new bloom blossoms with laughter out loud,
Growing friendships wild, making nature quite proud.

In this green revival, there's never a bore,
Every leaf whispers secrets, spirits to soar.
As bees don their suits in a buzz of delight,
Every moment shines brightly, from morning to night!

Blooms in the Corners

In every nook, a sprout so proud,
With tiny leaves that laugh out loud.
The cat tiptoes, sneaks a glance,
At dancing weeds, a wobbly dance.

The cactus dons a funny hat,
A prickly smile, what's up with that?
The ferns giggle in the light,
As leaves toss jokes, it's quite the sight.

Potted pals, they chat and cheer,
Sharing secrets that we can't hear.
And in the soil, worms weave tales,
Of garden antics, and silly fails.

So if you find some sprightly blooms,
Just know they're plotting funny dooms.
A botanical riot, on display,
With laughter sprouting every day!

Nature's Palette

The daisies giggle in the sun,
While violets argue about who won.
A sunflower wearing shades so cool,
Declares itself the garden's jewel.

The lilies waltz, a dance so grand,
While ants form lines, all in command.
The petunias swear they've seen it all,
From bees in tuxedos to bugs that crawl.

Pansies whisper jokes in spring,
As butterflies spread gossip, fluttering.
Nature's colors, a chaotic cheer,
Make every garden seem quite dear.

So grab your paintbrush, splash some hue,
In this wild world, there's work to do.
With every bloom, a laugh we find,
Nature's palette, both bold and blind!

Silhouettes of Green Dreams

The shadows dance upon the wall,
As leaves play tag, both big and small.
A trellis boasting tales of yore,
While creeping vines beg for one more score.

The broccoli wears a cape, quite bold,
To save the day, or so I'm told.
And dandelions, with laughter burst,
Whispering wishes, quenching their thirst.

A lizard strikes a funny pose,
Chasing tail, where the wild grass grows.
In this patch of dreams, laughter streams,
As nature whispers her playful themes.

So let's toast to the leafy friends,
Whose shenanigans never end.
In shadows cast by leafy seams,
We find a world of green dreams!

Breezy Lullabies from the Foliage

The breeze hums softly through the leaves,
As chatter floats, and laughter weaves.
A rustling tale that spins around,
In every branch, a joy is found.

The willows sway like silly fools,
Playing hopscotch with the garden tools.
The herbs gossip, plotting schemes,
In fragrant whispers, beneath moonbeams.

A butterfly flutters, slightly tipsy,
Questioning if the roots smell fishy.
As nectar flows, the bees agree,
It's quite a party, you'll see!

So let us dance with leafy friends,
In breezy tunes where laughter blends.
For every petal's giggle sweet,
Is nature's joy, a vibrant beat!

Whispers of Leaves

In the garden, squirrels dance,
Chasing shadows, take their chance.
With every leaf, a giggle sounds,
As nature plays in leafy bounds.

A frog leaps high, with tiny grace,
While butterflies join the race.
The sun peeks through, what a delight,
All join in for a leafy flight.

The flowers chuckle, colors bright,
Blowing kisses in pure light.
The breeze is filled with sweet delight,
Nature's laughter, pure and right.

So grab a seat, come take a peek,
In this green realm, we bask and speak.
With every rustle, a secret shared,
In leafy whispers, all hearts bared.

The Emerald Embrace

Under green arches, laughter grows,
As playful vines curl up like prose.
The ivy giggles, wriggling free,
In the embrace of a jolly spree.

Gnomes in hats, doing the cha-cha,
While daisies dream of a new tiara.
Sunflowers wink, so tall and grand,
In this green dance, they take a stand.

The wind teases the tiny buds,
With a tickle here, and a playful thud.
As petals pop, they laugh out loud,
In this emerald hug, we're all so proud.

So let's join in, what a merry sight,
In this playful twist of pure delight.
With every step, the greens will sway,
In laughter's arms, we'll dance and play.

Sanctuary of Vines

In a tangle of leaves, a party brews,
With chipmunks singing the latest blues.
The mossy floor, a comfy couch,
Where laughter echoes, soft as a slouch.

The vines play tricks, like friendly ghosts,
Wrapping around all who love to boast.
With every branch, a tickle or two,
Nature's giggle, ever so true.

In this leafy nook, the secrets flow,
Where even the squirrels join in the show.
The sunbeams dance, a golden ballet,
In this viney world, come laugh and play.

Let's toast to greenery with silly cheer,
And make new friends, far and near.
In this sanctuary, joys intertwine,
With every giggle, our hearts align.

Within Nature's Walls

Walls of green, what a sight to see,
A playful bound where we can be free.
The petals giggle, the trees make jokes,
As bumblebees roam with their funny pokes.

The hedgehogs waddle, so proud and bright,
While the tulips chatter, oh what a sight!
With every breeze, a tickle ensues,
In this funny realm, we can't lose.

The sky dons a hat, fluffy and wide,
While clouds join the fun, not one is shy.
In this leafy space, we all convene,
With laughter and cheer, all bask in green.

So come along, let's frolic and play,
In this jolly world, each whimsical day.
With every leaf, a smile unfolds,
In the warmth of nature, our hearts are bold.

Green Tapestry of Life

In the corner, a plant took the throne,
Adorned with a hat—who knew it could groan?
Cactus in armor, so prickly and proud,
Telling all visitors, "Come, join the crowd!"

Laughter erupts when the fern starts to sway,
A dance so peculiar, it leads hearts astray.
The vines are all tangled, like hair in a mess,
A jungle of chaos, oh what a success!

The parlor's alive with a green, vibrant hum,
As leaves gossip softly, "Look, here comes the fun!"
Each herb has a secret, whispered just so,
Sharing the tales of the sunlight's warm glow.

In this leafy kingdom, we stumble, we play,
Creating our stories in the silliest way.
With pots full of laughter, and soil full of cheer,
Life blooms in this haven—who needs to steer?

Breezes Through the Boughs

A gusty wind plays, tickling each leaf,
With branches that wiggle, it's quite the motif.
The oak, with its wisdom, chuckles with glee,
"Oh, why are you flailing? Just dance like me!"

The willow shakes hands with the sun's golden rays,
Seems she's the life of the garden soirées.
The roses gossip, the daisies will joke,
As they plot to surprise an old fence post bloke.

Squirrels in top hats convene on a branch,
With acorns as currency, taking a chance.
The lilac politely offers them tea,
But it's just purple pollen; oh, how it would be!

Breeze giggles and wraps us in fragrant delight,
As petals and laughter take flight in the night.
Dance, sway, and shimmer, we're free as can be,
In this lively green court, come join the jubilee!

Roots of Resilience

In the soil, deep down, where secrets entwine,
Roots tend to giggle, sipping sun like it's wine.
They wiggle and wriggle, plotting their schemes,
"Let's lift this ol' pot—we'll live out our dreams!"

Through cracks in the pavement, they poke and they pry,
"Who needs a garden? We're reaching the sky!"
The daisies all snicker, "Well, aren't they brave?
Can't wait for the day they avoid that big wave!"

An old tree trunk whispers its wisdom of yore,
"Grow wide and grow tall, but don't touch that door!"
While munching on leaves, a butterfly sneers,
"Can't we all lighten up? Let's drown out our fears!"

Come gather, dear friends, where the wild things convene,

Where resilience isn't just rooted, it's seen.
With laughter as fuel and fun in our veins,
We'll thrive through the seasons—through sunshine and rains!

The Hushed Chorus of Moss

In the shade, a green carpet, silent and sly,
Whispers of secrets as breezes drift by.
Damp and delightful, a cozy embrace,
Moss giggles softly in its fuzzy green lace.

A snail sings a ballad, slow as a dream,
As ladybugs clap in the style of a theme.
With cushions of green as they lounge by the brook,
The forest's old couch offers pages to look.

"Oh, join our soft symphony, hush now, don't peep,"
Says the lichen so prim, "We keep all the sheep!"
While shadows dance dreamily at dusk-turning-glow,
There's magic in silence—where would it not go?

So tread with great care on this tender terrain,
For the moss tells tall tales of joy and of pain.
In quietest corners, don't miss what you find,
The chorus of verdure sings sweetly, unlined.

Lush Echoes of Home

In corners where the plants all dance,
The ferns and vines take quite a chance.
A rubber tree dons socks of cheer,
While cacti giggle, never fear.

The sunbeams tickle leafy cheeks,
As spiders throw their little squeaks.
A parrot's playful serenade,
Turns every footstep to a parade.

The dirt's alive, it starts to hum,
As tomatoes laugh and start to sum.
The herbs are wise, with gossip rife,
Sharing secrets about our life.

In every pot, a riot reigns,
With friendly squash and playful grains.
The joy spills out in colors bright,
As laughter grows by day and night.

The Garden's Secret Heart

In the shadows where the radishes hide,
They hold parties and laugh with pride.
A carrot wears a tiny crown,
As veggie folks all come to town.

Busy bees come buzzing by,
With jokes that fly and never die.
They tickle blooms in a silly spree,
While daisies dance, just wait and see!

The spinach spins, it's quite a sight,
Declaring itself the veggie knight.
And peas will pop with double glee,
As they share tales with chamomile tea.

What secrets lie within this patch?
With every sprout a brand new catch.
In this realm, we giggle and flirt,
For giggling plants sure won't get hurt!

Flourish in Every Corner

A palm tree waves from its high perch,
While daisies dance with crafty lurch.
The ivy sings a cheeky song,
In this jolly jungle where we belong.

The broccoli just took a dive,
Claiming it's on a veggie high five.
While radishes roll in a happy tumble,
Mixed up in dirt, they start to fumble.

The lilies laugh as butterflies glance,
Amidst all this floral romance.
The basil twirls with rosemary,
Their friendship adds some flair to the scenery.

In every nook, a giggle swells,
As the garden's charm quite surely dwells.
For in this realm of playful hues,
There's laughter in every leafy muse.

Rooms of Verdant Dreams

In corners where the orchids sway,
The chives are plotting their display.
They whisper tales of muddy schemes,
In the warm embrace of leafy dreams.

In this abode where flowers shout,
The petals know what this is about.
A sunflower mocks the gardener's stance,
With its cheeky, sunny glance.

The ferns are whispering with delight,
Sharing stories from the night.
While mint steals snacks from the cupboard,
Demanding parties, oh so hubbubbed!

Through windows bright, the sunshine beams,
Filling every nook with golden gleams.
In this vibrant, giggling place,
Every bloom bursts with funny grace.

Mossy Nooks and Crannies

In corners where the shadows creep,
Moss holds secrets, but not too deep.
A squirrel once danced, slipped on a leaf,
And tumbled away, oh what a mischief!

Beneath the stairs, a tale unfolds,
Where old socks napped, or so I'm told.
The dust bunnies giggle, dance around,
I'm not alone, in this mess I've found!

A cactus mocks the feeble fern,
With spiky jabs, it's hard to learn.
But who needs wisdom when you can play,
In the nooks where greens decide to stay?

Entwined in laughter, plants conspire,
Their leafy pranks, sets hearts afire.
A home of cheer, with quirks so grand,
In every cranny, there's fun at hand!

Where Ivy Meets the Sky

Ivy in the window frames a view,
It tickles the clouds as if it knew.
A bee once mistook it for a dance,
Buzzing and whirling in a trance!

The branches wave, a friendly cheer,
Wishing for sunshine, and some cold beer.
A vine with gossip, tales of old,
And leaves that shimmer like bits of gold.

Up above, a bird made a nest,
Teasing the ivy, 'We're truly blessed!'
But when it rains, oh what a sight,
The ivy's curls, all drenched and tight!

With every twist and playful climb,
A comedy of plants, oh how sublime!
As ivy tickles the blue expanse,
A whimsical world, where we all dance.

Ferns in Forgotten Spaces

In the attic, where dust motes spin,
Ferns whisper secrets of where they've been.
Once a shoe, now a pot for green,
It laughs at the chaos, not shy to be seen!

Behind old books, they wiggle and sway,
Telling stories of yesterday's play.
With each little frond, they've got a jest,
Claiming that dust is their current quest!

A tapa-wearing toad hopped by once,
Challenged the fern, claimed a green dunce.
But in that space of forgotten dreams,
The laughter of ferns is louder than screams!

In crevices deep, they make their stand,
They know the secret of plant life's band.
For every forgotten nook, they adorn,
With jokes unknown, they keep us warm.

A Canopy of Comfort

Under the branches, my heart's a kite,
The leaves rustle softly, a pure delight.
A raccoon on the swing, takes a lazy nap,
While sunshine plays tag, and does a little clap.

The hammock sways, caught in sweet song,
Where fronds weave tales, and nothing feels wrong.
With every rustle, a chuckle is shared,
In this comfy cocoon, it's clear we are paired!

Above, the clouds throw a playful show,
As tiny leaves giggle, putting on a glow.
A picnic of dreams spreads out on the grass,
While laughter erupts from each cheeky pass.

In a world where greens gather and scheme,
Nestled beneath, we all can dream.
For in this place, with nature our guide,
Life is a joke, with joy on the side!

The Aroma of Earth and Growth

In corners where the weeds do dance,
A tomato plant wears a silly glance.
With carrots huddled, plotting their plot,
They giggle and wiggle in a sunny spot.

The lettuce leaps with a leafy cheer,
While radishes gossip what they overhear.
Sunflowers spin tales of bees in flight,
As they bask in the warmth of the morning light.

The compost pile starts to make jokes,
Telling the veggies, 'We're friends, not folks!'
With every earthworm twisting and twirling,
The garden's alive and joyfully swirling.

In this patch of chaos, laughter's the key,
Every seedling knows it's wild and free.
So, let's raise a toast with a berry-filled cup,
To nature's fun house where green things erupt!

Nooks of Nature's Splendor

In a nook where leafy critters reside,
A squirrel has claimed the biggest slide.
He squeaks with joy, eyes wide and bright,
As acorns tumble down, oh what a sight!

Ferns play hide and seek in the shade,
While flowers giggle, totally unafraid.
A snail in a shell takes a leisurely ride,
Chasing the shadows, oh what a glide!

Butterflies wear costumes, oh what a show,
As they dance with the breezes, to and fro.
It's a circus out here, no time for gloom,
Nature's just laughing, it's filled with bloom!

Rabbits are plotting a hop-scotch parade,
While bees buzz news, never delayed.
With every twist, turn, and curious glance,
Nature's a playground, let's join in the dance!

The Colors of Growth and Peace

In hues of green, the laughter spills,
Where daisies giggle on sunny hills.
A paintbox of petals, bright and bold,
Whispers secrets, soft and untold.

Hollyhocks strut in their fanciest dress,
While daisies drop lines, no need to impress.
A parade of colors march side by side,
In this riot of life, all creatures abide.

Even the weeds have a cheeky stunt,
Saying, 'We're here too! You better confront!'
They sing out loud, their voices quite brash,
In a colorful clash, what a fun little bash!

The garden's a canvas, painted with cheer,
Where nature's a joker, drawing us near.
So come grab a brush, let's paint with delight,
In our patch of joy, everything's right!

Flora's Embrace

In the arms of blooms, hugs come alive,
Dancing with petals, we all take a dive.
Bumblebees buzz with a rhythm so sweet,
While lilies throw parties, a colorful feat.

Daffodils tickle each passing bee,
'Come join our giggles, come laugh with me!'
As marigolds cheer from their cozy nook,
Together they gather, they read like a book.

With vines that whisper, they plot and they scheme,
To launch a surprise, oh, what a dream!
And in the twilight, it's quite the parade,
As shadows stretch long, and laughter cascades.

So here's to the blooms and their playful race,
In the garden of jests, we find our place.
With nature's embrace, there's joy to ignite,
In this whimsical world, everything feels right!

Harmony of Life in Green

In corners where the cactus sneezes,
And ivy dances on the breeze,
The fern is plotting, no power struggle,
While a turtle hums a happy jingle.

The parlor's bright with leafy dreams,
And laughter bubbles like sunlit streams,
A rubber plant occasionally yawns,
While daisies gossip on the lawns.

Charming chaos in every nook,
Spiders spinning tales like a book,
A secret world where shadows play,
And fake plants cheerfully betray.

From window ledge, the ivy peeks,
Morning sunlight, with yellow streaks,
A riot of green, a jubilant scene,
In our little home, where fun is seen.

Petals and Soft Shelters

The pillows burst with floral cheer,
As tulips tease my sleepy ear,
They whisper jokes, both wild and bright,
In dreams, they tickle, what a sight!

A hosta hat on Grandma's chair,
With daisies woven in her hair,
Each petal pitches in the fun,
As zinnias race in the sun.

Indoor jungles, a plush parade,
With every leaf, a prank is played,
The orchids prance in quirky boots,
While violets throw their funky roots.

Laughter mingles with morning dew,
As blossoms plan what they will do,
In a world of petals, soft and true,
We find the humor in green hues.

Verdant Refuge

Amidst the fronds, a squirrel's feast,
Where jasmine smells like popcorn, at least,
The ferns get jealous of the moss,
As cuttings trade their tales and gloss.

A rubber tree with a silly grin,
While every sprout invites a win,
Each twig has secrets, each vine's a tease,
In laughter's grip, like a soft breeze.

Pansies giggle in floral hats,
As insights sprout from chattering chats,
Here, lemonade flows from kale leaves,
With jokes exchanged behind the eaves.

This sanctuary, both lush and bright,
Invites the sun to share the light,
In this wild patch, so full of glee,
Life's funny quirks are plain to see.

The Calm of Naturally Adorned Spaces

A cactus, stiff yet full of flair,
Winks at succulents with pointed hair,
And grasshoppers leap in cheerful glee,
Beneath the smiles of each leafy tree.

Peeking through the curtains green,
A garden path that's seldom seen,
Where gnomes crack jokes to passing bees,
As tulips giggle in the breeze.

The pots are lined with snickers and cheer,
As thyme teases rosemary near,
And every shade of green's a wink,
In every corner, plants do think.

Such a calm space, filled with jest,
Nature's beauty is simply the best,
In harmony, they laugh and play,
Brightening up the dullest day.

Sips of Serenity Beneath Green Canopies

Under the canopy so bright,
Lemonade spills in flight.
Birds join in, they bring a tune,
Sipping shade beneath the moon.

Grasshoppers dance, a cheeky show,
Jumping high while we lie low.
Ants march past with tiny treats,
Declaring war on summer's sweets.

Laughter echoes, a playful scene,
Catching fireflies, oh so keen.
Petunias giggle, waving their stems,
While daisies chat with clover friends.

With every sip, a giggle spills,
Nature's joy, it simply thrills.
In this leafy shade we stay,
Finding fun in every way.

Whispers of Verdure

In tangled vines, secrets hide,
Mice play tag, then seek to glide.
Squirrels gossip about the breeze,
Telling tales among the trees.

Frogs recite their ribbit rhyme,
Bouncing beats in muddy grime.
The sun peeks through in a cheeky grin,
Who knew fun could live within?

Butterflies flaunt their fluttering wings,
Chasing dreams that nature brings.
Grass blades quiver, giggling bright,
As ladybugs take their flight.

The air is filled with laughter sweet,
In this green land, we find our beat.
With every whisper, joy unfolds,
Nature's humor never gets old.

Echoes of the Leafy Haven

In the burble of the brook's merry flow,
A wind chime laughs with every blow.
Tulips wink in a soft and bold hue,
While roses snicker at passing dew.

Chipmunks squabble over acorn prizes,
Each pouncing leap, a funny surprise.
Bumblebees buzz with a jolly hum,
Declaring summer has finally come!

The trees stretch wide, they're playing charades,
Branches waving in funny parades.
Sunlight flickers, a jester's dance,
Casting shadows that prance and prance.

Echoes of laughter, a joyful race,
In this leafy haven, we find our space.
Every moment, a joke well-timed,
In nature's lap, we're so well-climed.

Charmed by Nature's Bounty

Pixies prance on mushroom tops,
Gathering laughs and bubble pops.
Flowers sway in a giddy spin,
With every twist, giggles begin.

The ants are planning a grand parade,
While grasshoppers boast their serenade.
Caterpillars munch on leafy din,
Regaling tales as they sip gin!

Daisies play dress up, no fuss at all,
Wearing crowns at summer's ball.
Beetles pop in for a surprise,
Popping confetti, oh my, what a rise!

Nature's bounty, so wild and free,
Crafting charm for you and me.
In this green realm, we find delight,
As laughter fills the day and night.

Blossoms Behind Closed Doors

Behind closed doors, the plants convene,
With gossip and grumbles, they're quite the scene.
The orchids roll dice, ferns crack jokes,
While the tulips enlist in a game of hoax.

Pothos gives sass, a real cheeky flair,
While succulents snicker, without a care.
In this secret chamber, laughter releases,
As ivy entangles with stories of breezes.

The shy snake plant joins, timid but spry,
While the cacti throw shade, oh my, oh my!
In this leafy haven, it's quite the affair,
Where fretting for sunlight is banished with flair.

The Tranquil Grotto

In the tranquil grotto, the greens have a blast,
With vines playing tricks, oh, how they're steadfast.
A mossy old sofa, the best for a rest,
As laughter erupts at the comfiest guest.

The ferns tell tall tales of near-drowning dew,
While the dracaena downs a fizzy brew.
They swing on the curtains, oh what a sight,
Bouncing and giggling, till the stars are bright.

The peace lily winks, while the peace is maintained,
Yet chaos erupts, it's all quite entertained.
With leafy shenanigans, joy's painted on scenes,
In this hidden grotto, where nothing's routine.

Sanctuary of the Evergreen

In this sanctuary where the greens unite,
Jokes take root, putting troubles to flight.
With a bromeliad's laugh, and a jade's sly grin,
They plot little pranks, let the fun times begin!

The fiddle leaf fig, a bossy old sage,
Conducts the ballet on this leafy stage.
The laughter is rich, sprinkled with fun,
As the monsteras dance in the rays of the sun.

While whispering willows sing songs to the breeze,
The air is alive with giggles and tease.
In this evergreen sanctuary, joy classes commence,
As green-thumbed jokers weave humor dense.

Hideaways of the Leafy Realm

In the leafy realm, where the shadows play,
The plants spin tall tales that brighten the day.
Bamboo shoots whisper in mischievous tones,
While geraniums chuckle at their tiny loans.

A rubber plant boasts of its shiny good looks,
While critters in corners scurry like crooks.
A tile floor chimes with the laughter of greens,
As secrets are shared amongst spiky routines.

In hideaways bustling with nature's cheer,
Every green-based prattle turns trouble to clear.
So come join the fun where the verdant ones dwell,
In this giggling kingdom, all's perfectly swell!

Rooms Adorned in Nature's Tapestry

In the kitchen, ivy braids,
Basil buzzes while it serenades.
Cacti dance on window sills,
Gardening gloves and rolling hills.

In the living room, ferns express,
Whispers of green, a leafy mess.
Sofa cushions made of moss,
Who knew plants could be the boss?

The bathroom's wallpaper? Fern-ified,
Pothos in a bubble bath, dignified.
Rubber ducks with leafy hats,
Nature's laughter in all of that!

Every corner sprouts a giggle,
Plants and pillows, oh how they wiggle.
Nature's art, a vibrant boon,
Greenery's fun, a wild cartoon!

The Secret Garden Within

In the study, books pile high,
Paprika plants reach for the sky.
Pencil shavings, dirt and cheer,
The sage whispers, 'I'm glad you're here!'

Dining room with vines that weave,
Guests find salad leaves up their sleeve.
Chairs are draped in leafy lace,
It's a jungle party, what a place!

In the attic, moss starts to climb,
Dust bunnies dance, putting on a rhyme.
Old board games with green on the table,
Who knew vintage could be this able?

A secret spot with gnome and fern,
Every nook there's a twist to learn.
Nature giggles, chuckles, and sings,
In this leafy realm, everyone springs!

Shadows of the Evergreen

In the hallway, shadows lurk,
Plants playing hide-and-seek with a smirk.
Potted palms wave as we walk by,
Pretending to hold a plant-filled spy!

The bedroom whirs with leafy dreams,
Nightlights glow like moonlit beams.
Duvet's green, a jungle theme,
Snakes can curl, or so they seem!

In the attic, laughter's found,
With rubber plants dancing 'round.
Ceiling beams become a vine,
Tangled stories, all align!

Emerald shadows cast such cheer,
Whispering secrets anyone can hear.
Every leaf, a giggling sprite,
Shadows glow in the soft moonlight!

Green Heartbeats of Home

In the kitchen, herbs create,
Basil's fragrance sedates your fate.
Parsley jokes about its friends,
Chopping leaves, a laughter blend.

The hallway's lined with leafy cheer,
Every step's a plant-filled sphere.
From pothos to fairy lights,
Home is a garden full of delights!

Bathroom plants enjoy the splash,
Petunias giggle as you dash.
Toilet paper rolls with sprouts,
My, home has turned to plant-filled bouts!

In every room, there's something spry,
Green heartbeats make the spirit fly.
With every giggle, in every tome,
Laughter's essence is the heart of home!

Whispers Beneath the Skies

In the garden, a gnome takes a nap,
While broccoli plans a sneaky trap.
The carrots giggle, bouncing in place,
As lettuce throws a leafy embrace.

Clouds chuckle above, watching the show,
The weeds dance lightly, putting on a flow.
In this riot of green, all chaos abounds,
Nature's funny farm, where laughter resounds.

A squirrel in shades, struts like a star,
While daisies blush, unsure who they are.
The sun winks brightly, tickling the grass,
As flowers gossip as the minutes pass.

Each twig and petal shares a quick jest,
With roots that dig deeper, they jest and they zest.
So join in the fun, bring your green hat,
And laugh with the veggies, for that is where it's at!

The Canopy of Comfort

Underneath branches, shadows play tricks,
A puppy tries chasing a tree-full of sticks.
The daisies huddle, sipping on dew,
While moss has a party, just me and you.

Rabbits in costumes hop past on parade,
While sunflowers giggle at the silly charade.
Ferns hide their faces, so shy in the breeze,
As fluffs of dandelions float with such ease.

An old turtle mumbles, slow down the pace,
While ants in a line have no time to waste.
The wind whispers secrets, tickling delight,
On this leafy playground, everything's right.

So grab a good seat on the grass or a leaf,
And stay for the laughter, a grand old motif.
With nature our stage, we'll never grow bored,
In this cozy green haven, fun is our reward!

The Joy of Hidden Growth

In the cracks of the pavement, a sprout peeks out,
A bold little warrior, no room for doubt.
While daisies in armor guard their tall friends,
They giggle together, where nonsense transcends.

Behind every bud, there's a tale to be told,
Of mischievous mushrooms and daisies so bold.
As the violets murmur, they share naughty plans,
While sunbeams flash fingers at grasshopper bands.

A squirrel steals nuts while the plants just sigh,
They've learned the sly tricks of the bird up high.
But in this green chaos, together they roam,
In laughter and joy, they find their true home.

So here's to the verdant, the quirky, the fun,
May your heart sprout laughter, like seeds in the sun.
Here's dancing with petals, and singing with leaves,
In the joy of growth, everyone believes!

The Softness of Green Corners

In the corners of sunlight, the shadows embrace,
A gathering of greens, a whimsical space.
The clovers hold hands, in a circle of cheer,
While lazy grasshoppers humsongs in here.

The mint is all giggles, the thyme's full of sass,
A singing competition where nothing can pass.
With every fresh breeze, they sway to the beat,
And dance in the laughter of soft, comfy feet.

A butterfly flutters, thinking it's grand,
While a cucumber dreams of a rock band.
The ferns wave their arms, in a soft, leafy way,
As mushrooms and daisies join in the play.

So if you're in need of a chuckle or cheer,
Find solace in corners where silliness steers.
With blooms all around and a foot-tapping hum,
In this patch of delight, let the giggles just come!

Blossoms in the Attic

There's a plant in my attic, it thinks it's a tree,
Leaves waving wildly, even drinks my tea.
It's taken my slippers, claimed them for its nest,
Now it's the king, I'm merely a guest.

Cobwebs are curtains, dust bunnies play,
A party of peonies, hip-hip-hooray!
Each morning I find my old shoes adorned,
With daisies exploding, I'm slightly forlorn.

The bulbs have their meetings, they glow in delight,
Planning a journey to take over the night.
My old winter coat's now a place to hide,
In the middle of spring, what a wild ride!

Next time I check, there's a snail on the wall,
Holding a sign that says, "Welcome, y'all!"
This attic of mine is a botanical show,
With laughter and greenery stealing the glow.

Tranquil Canopy

In the corner, a fern wears a tiny hat,
Sipping on sunlight, imagine that!
The sofa is cushioned with pillows of moss,
Where my cat claims her throne, oh what a loss!

The curtains are vines, creeping up to the sky,
Dancing with shadows when breezes pass by.
Potted banana plants throwing shade everywhere,
Chasing the dust bunnies with wild, frizzy hair.

I once lost a sandwich in bright green jungle,
Now it's thriving in soil, oh what a fumble!
The laughter of daisies fills up the room,
While I ponder the fate of that poor slice of gloom.

Who knew that the herbs were real-life comedians?
Telling tall tales of their plant expeditions.
So here in my haven, where laughter takes flight,
Life's uproarious dance keeps me feeling quite right.

The Verdant Nest

There's a cactus that laughs, it's full of good cheer,
When I tickle its spines, it seems to persevere.
My garden's a circus, with zinnias that sing,
While tomatoes debate on the state of spring.

Sunflowers act silly, with heads in the clouds,
Throwing shade at the daisies, bunching up crowds.
A leprechaun's whiskers made out of thyme,
Tell jokes to the beans, oh, they're having a time!

In pots full of chaos, my plants play charades,
Me giving the hints, while my sanity fades.
But laughter's contagious, I can't help but grin,
With a dance from the herbs, let the fun begin!

So raise up a cup of my botanical brew,
To the creatures and critters that grow and that grew.
In this green-tastic world, where the humor is keen,
Life's just a sitcom, where all's evergreen!

Overgrown Memories

My backyard's a jungle, what happened to grass?
The weeds are all laughing, "We'll never let pass!"
A gnome on my lawn, with a drink in his hand,
Winks at the roses, who make quite the band.

The hydrangeas gossip, share tales of the moon,
"My blooms are the biggest, they'll be here 'til June!"
While broccoli stalks hold a fashion parade,
In colorful attire, they strut unafraid.

My veggies are plotting a grand dinner scene,
Debating the merits of being organic.
But amidst all the chaos, I sip on my tea,
Chuckling at nature's hilarious spree.

So here's to my garden, with memories spry,
Where laughter grows tall and the humor won't die.
Every leaf is a friend in this wild, leafy dome,
In the circus of green, I've found my true home.

A Symphony of Growing Things

In the kitchen, herbs collide,
Basil winks, while thyme takes pride.
The cucumber's doing breakdance moves,
As carrots groove to the rock 'n' grooves.

Potatoes sing, they just can't stop,
While lettuce is caught in a leafy hop.
Peppers jam with style and flair,
A veggie concert, without a care.

The sunflowers sway with all their might,
Requesting solos, oh what a sight!
Chanting roots beneath the floor,
Nature's band, who could ask for more?

So gather 'round for fun and cheer,
Nature's performance, loud and clear.
In this garden, we dance and spin,
A symphony where all can win.

Gardens that Hold Secrets

Behind the fence, secrets lie,
A gnome whispers as bunnies fly.
Tomatoes giggle, hiding their blush,
While radishes turn to avoid the rush.

The scarecrow tells tales of the night,
How worms learn to tango, oh what a sight!
Mint leaves whisper, 'Shh, don't you know?'
What happens in soil, must never show!

Chickens cluck riddles with a cheeky grin,
They peep about puddles that hold the spin.
The daisies are plotting a garden ball,
While carrots compete to grow above all.

In this patch, mischief abounds,
Secrets grow in the soft, rich grounds.
Join us there, if you dare to peek,
At the funny games these greens seek.

Foliage's Gentle Touch

Leaves tickle toes as we roam about,
Whispers of greens, nature's shout.
Creeping vines sneak up with glee,
Making friends with the old oak tree.

The ivy chats with the wooden bench,
While fronds re-enact a circus wrench.
Petunias giggle, waving from the bed,
As sunbeams tap-dance overhead.

Cabbages play peek-a-boo with the sun,
Each time it shines, they have such fun.
Lettuce spins in a soft, warm breeze,
Challenging flowers to laugh with ease.

So take a stroll, feel the gentle sway,
In this green realm, bright as a play.
With each step, joy takes flight,
In the garden's soft, leafy light.

Mossy Dreams Beneath Our Feet

Moss grows thick like a fuzzy rug,
Where squirrels may snooze and feel snug.
A toadstool jumps with a springy flair,
Whispering wishes to the cool, damp air.

Slip past the ferns, beneath the trees,
Where mushrooms giggle in the soft breeze.
They hide their laughter under a cap,
Creating a theater, a nature map.

The snails parade in their shiny shells,
Sharing gossip with the woodland spells.
A critter conga along the lane,
In this mossy wonder, there's never a stain!

So wander here, in green delight,
With creatures capering, oh what a sight!
Dreams of moss, where fun won't cease,
In the plush carpets, we find our peace.

Echoes in the Canopy

In the kitchen, vines entwine,
They sneak up high like they own the line.
A fruit bowl dances, quite in glee,
While ants debate on who gets the spree.

Cactus in slippers, what a sight!
Singing with a fern deep into the night.
The sink is gurgling tunes of cheer,
As green leaves giggle, loud and clear.

A parrot jives on the countertop,
Gray squirrels join in, please don't stop!
Raisin toast and plants chat away,
Making breakfast like it's a Broadway play.

When guests arrive, they can't believe,
Lettuce wearing hats is hard to conceive.
Hose pipes throw a grand old bash,
While everybody tumbles in a splash.

Ferns in the Foyer

The start of the tale is fancy sprigs,
Dancing in the hallway, doing jigs.
Doormats with moss are hard to ignore,
Welcoming guests to a leafy decor.

Potted pals give a sly, green wink,
While shadows play as they start to blink.
Dust bunnies tango with little roots,
And carrots giggle in their tiny suits.

Driftwood and daisies hold a ball,
When everyone's in, it's a wild free-for-all.
Ferns gossip as they twirl their fronds,
Trading secrets like enchanted wands.

At the end of the night, a truce is found,
As plants are napping, lounging around.
Earthy aromas fill the air,
Creating smiles that they gladly share.

Ivy Climbing Dreams

Ivy plots with a twinkle in its eye,
Wishing and dreaming to touch the sky.
Ladder of leaves reaching so tall,
Whispering wishes to the hallway wall.

A sloth on the shelf wears a viney crown,
While orchids laugh at the sofa down.
Each pillow is a cloud, they giggle by,
As the drapes sway slow, like birds in the sky.

Plants play poker under the light,
Cacti in shades wearing smiles so bright.
Getting lost in green games all day,
Tangled in laughter, they dance and sway.

When night falls softly, dreams take flight,
The ivy whispers secrets to the night.
A raucous cheer erupts from below,
As green friends met in dreams overflow.

Glistening Leaves at Dusk

At dusk the scene is quite absurd,
Leaves are gossiping, each a word.
Slippery snails slide with such flair,
While shadows stretch and dance in the air.

A bunny hops in with a bow tie on,
As crickets croon their twilight song.
The light wraps low like a cozy quilt,
Warming the foliage that's finely built.

Twinkling lights made of firefly wreaths,
Illuminate antics among the leaves.
A squirrel's disco moves leave us stunned,
While the willow tree just shakes and runs.

As the moonlight bathes the scene in glow,
Each petal winks, an audience aglow.
Laughter drifts through the velvety night,
In a place where green brings pure delight.

www.ingramcontent.com/pod-product-compliance
Lightning Source LLC
Chambersburg PA
CBHW070316120526
44590CB00017B/2702